Divinity Book Second Chapter
By Ladarius Murray

ISBN 979-8-89569-459-6

Chapter 1: The Beginning of the Journey

The sun dipped low over the horizon, casting a golden glow across the city. In the distance, the hum of traffic mixed with the faint sound of laughter from a nearby park. It was the end of another school day, and students hurried home, eager to leave behind the day's worries. But for Amara, the end of the school day marked the beginning of a different kind of challenge.

Amara stood at the entrance of Greenwood High, her textbooks clutched tightly against her chest. Her dark, curly hair framed her face, and her eyes held a quiet determination. She had always been the type to blend into the background, focusing on her studies and keeping out of trouble. But today, something felt different.

As she walked down the hallway, she couldn't help but overhear snippets of conversation between her classmates. Most of them were excited about the upcoming weekend, but there was also a lot of talk about the big chemistry test on Friday. Amara had always excelled in chemistry, and she knew she was ready for the test. But the chatter around her hinted at something more—a plan to cheat.

"Did you hear? Jake's got the answers to the test. If you're in, meet in the parking lot after school," one girl whispered to her friend.

Amara's heart sank. Jake was one of the most popular guys in school, and he had a reputation for getting what he wanted, no matter the cost. She knew that getting involved in something like this could jeopardize everything she'd worked for—her grades, her reputation, and most importantly, her integrity.

She kept walking, her pace quickening as she tried to shake off the uneasy feeling that settled in her stomach. When she finally reached her locker, she found Sofia waiting for her.

Sofia was the opposite of Amara in many ways—outgoing, artistic, and unafraid to stand out. Her long, dark hair was pulled back in a messy ponytail, and her hands were smudged with charcoal from her latest art project.

Meanwhile, on the other side of town, Liam was dealing with his own set of challenges. He stood in the middle of the football field, sweat dripping down his face as he stared at the goalposts. His coach had been pushing him harder than ever, and the pressure was starting to take its toll.

"Come on, Liam! You've got to give it everything you've got!" Coach Thompson shouted from the sidelines. "You want to make your dad proud, don't you?"

Liam winced at the mention of his father. His dad had been a football star in his youth, and everyone expected Liam to follow in his footsteps. But no matter how hard he tried, it never seemed to be enough. The weight of those expectations hung heavy on his shoulders, making it hard for him to enjoy the game he once loved.

He took a deep breath and ran toward the goalposts, putting all his strength into the kick. The ball sailed through the air and landed squarely between the posts. The coach nodded in approval, but Liam felt no sense of accomplishment. It was just another task, another expectation met.

As he left the field and headed home, Liam couldn't help but wonder if this was all there was. Was his life destined to be a series of goals met and expectations fulfilled? Or was there something more, something that he was missing?

Across town, Sofia sat at her desk, sketching the outline of a new piece. Art was her escape, the one place where she felt truly free. But even in her art, she couldn't escape the pressure from her family. They had always wanted her to pursue something more "practical," like medicine or law. But Sofia couldn't imagine giving up her passion.

Her phone buzzed, interrupting her thoughts. It was a text from her mom, reminding her about a meeting with a college admissions counselor that evening. Sofia sighed, putting down her pencil. She knew the conversation would revolve around which colleges had the best pre-med programs, not the best art schools.

As she prepared to leave, she glanced at the sketchbook, filled with half-finished drawings and ideas. They were all pieces of herself, pieces that she wasn't sure anyone else would understand.

And then there was Ethan. He sat alone in his room, surrounded by computer parts and blueprints. He was working on his latest invention—a drone that could deliver packages autonomously. But no matter how many times he tried, something always seemed to go wrong. The drone would wobble, lose balance, or crash before reaching its destination.

Ethan's parents had always been supportive, but he could see the doubt in their eyes. They wanted him to succeed, but they didn't really understand his passion for technology. They worried that he was wasting his time on something that might never amount to anything.

As he stared at the broken drone in front of him, Ethan wondered if they were right. Maybe he was just chasing a dream that would never come true. But a small part of him refused to give up. He knew he had something special, something that could change the world—if only he could figure out how to make it work.

Chapter 2: The Crossroads

The days leading up to the chemistry test passed in a blur for Amara. Everywhere she went, it seemed like the temptation to take the easy way out was growing stronger. In the hallways, in the cafeteria, even in the whispers exchanged during class—everyone seemed to be talking about Jake's plan.

Amara had always prided herself on doing things the right way. Her parents had raised her to value hard work and honesty, and she knew they would be disappointed if she compromised those values. But the pressure was mounting, and doubt began to creep in.

On Wednesday, after the final bell rang, Amara lingered by her locker, her thoughts swirling. She was just about to leave when she noticed Rachel, a girl from her chemistry class, heading her way.

"Amara, wait up!" Rachel called, her tone casual but her eyes sharp.

Amara paused, a knot tightening in her stomach. Rachel was one of those girls who always seemed to know what was going on, who was friends with everyone but never really close to anyone.

"So," Rachel began, leaning against the locker next to Amara's, "you ready for the big test on Friday?"

Amara nodded, unsure where this conversation was headed. "Yeah, I've been studying a lot."

Rachel smiled, but it didn't reach her eyes. "That's great, but you know... there's an easier way to ace it."

Amara's heart skipped a beat. She knew exactly what Rachel was talking about, but she tried to play dumb. "What do you mean?"

Rachel glanced around to make sure no one was listening. “Jake’s got the answers. He’s selling them after school tomorrow. Everyone’s doing it—no harm, no foul. Just a little insurance, you know?”

Amara felt a cold wave of anxiety wash over her. She had heard rumors, but hearing it directly made it real. “I don’t know, Rachel. That doesn’t seem right.”

Rachel’s smile faltered for a moment, but she quickly recovered. “Come on, Amara. You’re one of the smartest people in our class. You’ve got nothing to lose. Besides, do you really want to risk your grade over something so... small?”

Amara looked down at her hands, her mind racing. She knew cheating was wrong, but the fear of failing—or even just not doing as well as she hoped—was gnawing at her.

“I’ll think about it,” she said finally, not meeting Rachel’s eyes.

Rachel shrugged. “Suit yourself. Just don’t take too long to decide. Jake’s got limited slots, and once they’re gone, they’re gone.”

As Rachel walked away, Amara felt a heavy weight settle on her chest. She knew she had a choice to make, but no matter what she decided, it felt like she was about to lose something important.

***

Meanwhile, Liam sat on the edge of his bed, staring at the framed photo of his father that hung on the wall. In the picture, his dad was young, strong, and full of life, holding up a trophy with a triumphant grin. It was taken just after he had won the state championship in football, the same championship Liam's team was now working toward.

Liam sighed, running a hand through his damp hair. Practice had been brutal today, and Coach Thompson had been relentless, pushing him to be faster, stronger, better. "You've got to live up to your father's legacy," the coach had said more than once.

But the pressure was starting to crush him. Liam loved football, but lately, it felt more like a burden than a passion. The expectations were too high, and no matter how hard he tried, he never felt like he was good enough.

As he lay back on his bed, his phone buzzed with a message from his teammate, Jordan.

"Yo, Liam. Got something that can give us an edge" Jordan said "Meet us after practice tomorrow. Don't tell Coach."

Liam frowned, sitting up. He had heard whispers in the locker room about some of the guys taking supplements to boost their performance. It wasn't exactly illegal, but it wasn't right either.

His mind flashed back to the talk his dad had given him when he first started playing football. "Liam, it's not just about winning. It's about how you play the game. Integrity, son—that's what makes a real man."

But was integrity enough? Liam wondered. Could he really meet everyone's expectations by just playing fair? Or was it time to start doing whatever it took to win, even if it meant compromising his values?

The decision weighed heavily on him, and as he drifted off to sleep, the words of his father echoed in his mind, battling against the voices of doubt.

***

At a small café in the heart of the city, Sofia sat across from her mother, listening as the college admissions counselor droned on about the best pre-med programs in the country. Sofia's sketchbook lay untouched beside her, a stark contrast to the neatly organized brochures spread out on the table.

"We really think Sofia has the potential to excel in a rigorous academic environment," the counselor was saying. "With her grades, she could easily get into a top-tier school."

Her mother nodded enthusiastically. "That's exactly what we want for her. She's always been so talented in science."

Sofia forced a smile, her mind miles away. Science was fine, but it wasn't her passion. Art was where her heart truly lay, but she hadn't found the courage to tell her mother that. Every time she tried, the words stuck in her throat.

The counselor handed her another brochure, this one featuring a prestigious pre-med program. Sofia glanced at it briefly before slipping it into her bag. She knew what her mother expected of her, but the more they talked about her future, the more she felt like she was being pulled in a direction that wasn't her own.

After the meeting, they walked out into the cool evening air. Sofia's mother was talking excitedly about the options they had discussed, but Sofia's thoughts were elsewhere. She couldn't shake the feeling that she was slowly losing herself, that with each passing day, she was drifting further away from the person she wanted to be.

When they passed by the café's outdoor seating area, Sofia spotted Amara sitting alone, staring down at a piece of paper in her hands. Something in her expression made Sofia pause.

"Mom, I'll catch up with you later, okay?" Sofia said, giving her mother a quick kiss on the cheek before heading over to Amara's table.

Amara looked up as Sofia approached, her eyes widening in surprise. "Hey, Sofia. What are you doing here?"

"Just had a meeting with a college counselor," Sofia replied, pulling out a chair and sitting down. "What about you? You look like you've got a lot on your mind."

Amara hesitated, then sighed. "Yeah, I do. I'm... trying to figure out what to do about this test on Friday."

Sofia raised an eyebrow. "The chemistry test? You'll be fine, Amara. You're one of the smartest people I know."

"It's not that," Amara said quietly, glancing around to make sure no one was listening. "Rachel told me that Jake's selling the answers. She said everyone's doing it."

Sofia's expression darkened. "And you're thinking about it?"

"I don't know," Amara admitted. "I know it's wrong, but... what if I don't do well? What if I disappoint my parents?"

Sofia reached across the table and squeezed Amara's hand. "You're not going to disappoint anyone, Amara. You've worked hard for this, and you're going to do great—without cheating."

Amara looked up, meeting Sofia's gaze. "Thanks, Sofia. I just... needed to hear that."

"No problem," Sofia said with a smile. "Besides, you're better than that. Don't let anyone convince you otherwise."

As they sat together, Amara felt a little of the weight lift from her shoulders. Maybe she wasn't alone in this after all.

***

Back at his house, Ethan was hunched over his desk, surrounded by the remnants of his latest failed drone. The room was a mess of wires, circuit boards, and tools, but Ethan barely noticed. He was too focused on figuring out where he had gone wrong.

He had been at it for hours, tweaking and adjusting, but nothing seemed to work. The drone still couldn't fly properly, and with each failure, Ethan's frustration grew.

Just as he was about to give up for the night, his phone buzzed with a notification. It was a new video from one of his favorite tech YouTubers, a guy who specialized in troubleshooting and DIY projects.

Ethan hesitated, then clicked on the video. As the YouTuber explained how to diagnose common drone issues, something clicked in Ethan's mind. He had been approaching the problem all wrong.

Suddenly energized, Ethan grabbed a screwdriver and started making adjustments, following the advice from the video. He reworked the drone's balance system, adjusted the propellers, and recalibrated the sensors.

When he finally finished, he held his breath and powered up the drone. It whirred to life, hovering steadily in the air. A grin spread across Ethan's face as the drone performed a perfect loop before landing smoothly on his desk.

For the first time in days, Ethan felt a surge of confidence. Maybe he wasn't wasting his time after all. Maybe he really could make something of this.

***

As the evening drew to a close, each of the four teens lay in bed, their thoughts racing.

Chapter 3: Testing the Waters

Amara sat at her desk, the test paper in front of her. She could feel the tension in the room, the silence broken only by the scratching of pencils on paper. Her heart raced as she worked through each problem, resisting the urge to glance around and see who might have taken the easy way out. Every question felt like a mountain to climb, but with each one she completed, her confidence grew.

When the bell finally rang, she handed in her test and walked out of the classroom, her mind buzzing with uncertainty. But as she left, she caught a glimpse of Rachel's anxious expression, and something shifted inside her. Amara realized that no matter the outcome, she had done the right thing. That was something no grade could take away from her.

***

Liam stood in the locker room, staring at the small bottle of supplements Jordan had handed him. The label promised increased stamina and muscle growth, the kind of boost that could make all the difference on the field. But something about it felt wrong.

He thought of his father's words—integrity, character, playing the game the right way. Could he really betray those values for a shortcut? His heart pounded as he tightened his grip on the bottle.

"Yo, Liam, you coming?" Jordan called from the doorway, a grin on his face.

Liam looked up, then down at the bottle in his hand. Without a word, he walked over to the trash can and dropped it in. "Yeah," he said, meeting Jordan's surprised gaze. "I'm coming."

As they headed out to the field, Liam felt a sense of relief. He didn't need shortcuts. He had what it took to succeed—on his own terms.

***

Sofia sat in her room, her hands trembling as she finished her application to the art competition. Her heart raced with a mix of fear and excitement. For the first time, she was taking a step toward her own dreams, not just the ones her mother had laid out for her.

She saved the application and leaned back in her chair, staring at the ceiling. What if her mother found out? What if she was rejected? The doubts swirled in her mind, but a small voice inside her urged her on.

Sofia took a deep breath and clicked "Submit." The fear was still there, but now, so was something else—hope.

***

Ethan couldn't stop smiling as he watched his drone hover effortlessly in the air. The adjustments he had made were working perfectly, and for the first time, he felt like he was truly onto something.

He spent the next few days fine-tuning the design, pushing the limits of what the drone could do. His progress didn't go unnoticed—one of his teachers, Mr. Delgado, saw him working after class one day and stopped to watch.

" That's impressive work, Ethan," Mr. Delgado said, nodding at the drone. "Have you ever thought about entering it into the regional science fair?"

Ethan's eyes widened. He hadn't even considered that. "I... I guess I could."

"You should. I think you've got something special here," Mr. Delgado said with a smile. "Keep it up."

As Mr. Delgado walked away, Ethan felt a surge of pride. Maybe he really could make something of this. And maybe, just maybe, he was finally starting to believe in himself.

***

As the week went on, the four teens continued to face their challenges head-on, each of them growing stronger in their own way. Little did they know, their paths were about to cross in ways that would change their lives forever.

Chapter 4: Bonds Begin to Form

The following week at school was buzzing with excitement. The annual school fair was just around the corner, and this year, the principal had announced a new initiative: a student-led project competition. The challenge was to create something innovative that could benefit the school or the local community.

Amara was in the library after school, flipping through a textbook when she overheard Mr. Delgado talking to another teacher.

"The principal is really excited about this competition," Mr. Delgado said. "He wants the students to come up with something that shows creativity, teamwork, and real-world impact."

Amara's ears perked up. She had been looking for a way to challenge herself, to do something that went beyond just getting good grades. Maybe this was it.

Later that day, she found Sofia sitting by the art room, sketching in her notebook. Amara hesitated for a moment, then approached her.

"Hey, Sofia," Amara said, trying to sound casual. "Did you hear about the school project competition?"

Sofia looked up, her eyes brightening. “Yeah, it sounds pretty cool. Are you thinking of entering?”

“I was, actually,” Amara admitted. “But I’m not sure what to do. I was hoping… maybe we could work together?”

Sofia smiled. “I’d love that. Maybe we could combine our skills—science and art. We could create something really unique.”

As they brainstormed, an idea began to take shape. What if they designed an educational exhibit that could teach students about environmental science in a fun and interactive way? Sofia could create the visuals, while Amara handled the scientific content.

The more they talked, the more excited they became. But they both knew they would need more help to make their vision a reality.

***

Meanwhile, Liam was in the gym, running drills with his teammates. After practice, he sat on the bleachers, catching his breath, when he noticed Ethan tinkering with his drone in the corner of the gym.

Liam had always been curious about Ethan's projects but had never had a reason to approach him. Today, though, something nudged him to walk over.

"Hey, Ethan," Liam said, waving as he approached. "That drone's looking pretty slick. What are you working on?"

Ethan looked up, surprised but pleased to see Liam showing interest. "Just making some adjustments for the science fair. Mr. Delgado thinks I should enter it."

Liam nodded, impressed. "That's awesome. You know, I was thinking... There's this school project competition coming up. Amara and Sofia are working on something, but they could use someone with your skills."

Ethan's curiosity was piqued. "What kind of project?"

Liam explained their idea of creating an educational exhibit. "They need someone who can handle the tech side of things—maybe you could design an interactive model or something. I could help with the physical setup and logistics."

Ethan thought about it for a moment, then smiled. "That sounds like a challenge. I'm in."

***

The next day, the four of them gathered in the library to discuss their project. Amara and Sofia explained their idea in more detail, and Ethan immediately began brainstorming ways to bring it to life.

“We could use augmented reality,” Ethan suggested. “It’s cutting-edge tech that could make the exhibit interactive. Students could point their phones at different parts of the exhibit, and animations or additional information could pop up.”

“That sounds amazing,” Sofia said, her eyes lighting up. “I can design the visuals to work with the AR. We could create an experience that’s both educational and engaging.”

Liam, who had been listening quietly, spoke up. “I can help with the physical setup—building the stands, arranging the space, making sure everything runs smoothly on the day of the fair.”

Amara smiled, feeling a sense of pride in their team. Each of them brought something unique to the table, and together, they were creating something that none of them could have done alone.

As they worked together over the next few weeks, the group began to bond in ways they hadn’t expected.

-Amara was surprised to find that Sofia’s creativity inspired her to think outside the box in her scientific explanations.

-Sofia found that working with Amara helped her add depth and meaning to her artwork, something she had been struggling with.
-Liam enjoyed the challenge of managing the project, using the leadership skills he had developed in football to keep things on track.
-Ethan relished the opportunity to apply his technical skills to something real and meaningful, and he appreciated how his teammates valued his contributions.

One afternoon, after a long day of working on the exhibit, they all decided to grab a snack at the café where Sofia and Amara had met before. As they sat around the table, chatting and laughing, it became clear that they were no longer just classmates—they were becoming friends.

They began to open up to each other about their lives, their struggles, and their dreams. Amara shared how much pressure she felt to always be perfect in her parents' eyes. Sofia talked about her secret passion for art and the fear of disappointing her mother. Liam admitted that living up to his father's legacy was starting to feel like an impossible task. Ethan spoke about his insecurities and how he often felt like he didn't fit in.

As they listened to each other, they realized that they weren't as different as they had thought. They all had their own battles to fight, but they didn't have to fight them alone.

The next few weeks flew by as they worked tirelessly on their project. They faced setbacks—technical glitches, design challenges, and time constraints—but each time, they came together to find a solution.

As the school fair approached, the exhibit was finally coming together. The centerpiece was a large interactive model of a sustainable city, with different sections that highlighted various aspects of environmental science. The AR features added a layer of interactivity that brought the exhibit to life, making it both educational and fun.

On the day of the fair, as they put the finishing touches on their exhibit, Amara looked around at her teammates. They had started this project as acquaintances, but now, they were a team. More than that, they were friends.

And as they stood back to admire their work, they knew that no matter what happened at the competition, they had already won something far more important.

Chapter 5: Facing Adversity

The day of the school fair had finally arrived. The gym was filled with the energy of students, teachers, and visitors excitedly moving from booth to booth, admiring the different projects. Amara, Sofia, Liam, and Ethan stood proudly in front of their exhibit—a vibrant, interactive display of their sustainable city model, complete with augmented reality features that made the content come alive.

Everything seemed to be going perfectly. Their teamwork had paid off, and visitors were impressed by how the exhibit blended science, art, and technology. Even the principal stopped by to compliment their work. But, as the crowd around their exhibit grew, so did the pressure.

Amara was explaining the AR features to a group of parents when she noticed something strange—one of the screens wasn't responding. She tried refreshing it, but nothing happened. Her heart began to race as more people gathered around, waiting for the next demonstration.

"Ethan," she called out quietly, not wanting to cause a scene. "Something's wrong with the system."

Ethan rushed over, his brow furrowing as he checked the setup. "That's weird. It was working fine earlier." He began troubleshooting, but the problem only seemed to worsen. The AR features were glitching, and the animations wouldn't load properly.

The group's confidence began to falter as the technical issues piled up. Sofia's beautifully designed visuals were stuck, and the flow of their presentation was falling apart. Liam, usually calm and composed, was struggling to manage the growing crowd of people waiting to see their exhibit. The tension in the air was palpable.

"I think we overloaded the system," Ethan muttered, his hands flying across the keyboard, trying to reboot the software. "It wasn't built to handle this many users at once."

Amara could feel the weight of the situation bearing down on her. They had worked so hard for this moment, and now, it was slipping away. She glanced at Sofia, who looked equally panicked, and at Liam, who was pacing back and forth, trying to calm the crowd.

Sofia, standing off to the side, felt helpless. Her designs were frozen on the screen, and all the hours she had spent perfecting them seemed wasted. She looked at Amara, her eyes wide with frustration. "What are we going to do?"

Amara took a deep breath, trying to stay calm. She knew that panicking wouldn't solve anything, but the pressure was building. All around them, the other exhibits seemed to be running smoothly, making their malfunction all the more glaring.

Just as things were beginning to feel hopeless, a voice cut through the tension.

"Guys, it's okay," Liam said firmly, stepping forward. "We've faced worse. Let's think this through."

Ethan looked up from his laptop, sweat beading on his forehead. "I'm trying to fix it, but it's going to take time."

Liam nodded, then turned to Amara and Sofia. "We can't stop now. We need to keep the crowd engaged while Ethan works on the tech. Amara, you're great at explaining things. You handle the science. Sofia, you walk people through the visuals."

Sofia looked unsure. "But they won't be able to see the AR animations..."

"They don't need to," Liam said, his voice steady. "Your artwork is amazing on its own. Just talk them through it. We've got this."

Amara swallowed her nerves and nodded. She could feel the weight of the situation, but Liam's calm confidence gave her a sliver of hope. "Okay," she said, turning to the crowd. "Let's keep this going."

With Liam directing the flow of people and Ethan working frantically in the background, Amara began explaining the science behind their exhibit, describing how sustainable cities could help combat climate change. Sofia joined in, pointing to her designs and explaining the thought process behind each section. Slowly, they began to regain the attention of the audience.

As they spoke, something remarkable happened. The crowd, initially disappointed by the technical issues, became captivated by the passion with which Amara and Sofia presented their project. Without the reliance on technology, the two girls began to shine in their own right, connecting with the visitors on a more personal level.

Ethan, meanwhile, was making progress. After what felt like an eternity, he managed to reboot the system, and the AR features slowly came back to life. When the animations finally flickered onto the screens, a wave of relief washed over the group.

"Got it!" Ethan exclaimed, stepping back triumphantly as the crowd gasped at the return of the interactive elements.

But by then, something had shifted. The technical problems had forced the group to rely on their own skills and creativity rather than on the technology they had built. And in doing so, they had discovered a new kind of strength—a strength that came from their teamwork, their resilience, and their ability to adapt under pressure.

As the day went on, more and more visitors flocked to their exhibit, not just for the technology, but to hear the team explain their work.

Amara's knowledge of science, Sofia's artistic vision, Liam's leadership, and Ethan's technical expertise all came together in a way that was far more powerful than any one of them could have achieved alone.

***

At the end of the day, when the crowd had finally thinned out, the group sat down together in a quiet corner of the gym, exhausted but triumphant.

"I can't believe we pulled that off," Amara said, still catching her breath.

"It was a close call," Sofia added with a tired smile. "But Liam, you kept us from falling apart."

Liam shrugged, trying to play it cool, though he couldn't hide the grin on his face. "We're a team. We don't give up."

Ethan leaned back, wiping the sweat from his forehead. "I'm just glad the system came back online. But honestly, you guys didn't even need it. You killed it out there."

Amara, Sofia, and Liam all looked at each other, realizing that Ethan was right. The technology had been a bonus, but what had really made their exhibit a success was their ability to come together and adapt to the situation.

"We made a pretty good team, didn't we?" Amara said softly.

"The best," Sofia agreed, nodding.

Liam grinned, glancing around at his friends. "So, what's next?"

They all laughed, but deep down, each of them knew that this was just the beginning. They had faced their first real test together and had come out stronger on the other side. Whatever challenges lay ahead, they were ready to take them on—together.

Chapter 6: Strength in Unity

The school fair was over, but the impact of their experience lingered long after. Amara, Sofia, Liam, and Ethan returned to their regular routines, but something had changed. They were no longer just classmates working on a project; they had become a tight-knit team. Their bond had been forged through adversity, and it was stronger than any of them had anticipated.

A week later, the principal called a special assembly to announce the winners of the project competition. The gym was packed with students, all eager to see who would take home the top prize. Amara, Sofia, Liam, and Ethan sat together, their hearts pounding in anticipation.

When the principal finally took the stage, he praised all the students for their creativity and hard work. As he began to announce the winners, the tension in the room grew. Third place went to a group that had created a sustainable garden for the school grounds. Second place was awarded to a team that had developed a mobile app for tracking students' environmental impact.

"And now," the principal said, his voice booming through the microphone, "the first place in this year's project competition goes to... the Sustainable City AR Exhibit, created by Amara, Sofia, Liam, and Ethan!"

The gym erupted in applause. The four friends exchanged shocked but ecstatic glances as they made their way to the stage. Standing in front of the entire school, they received their trophy—a symbol of their teamwork, resilience, and creativity.

As they walked off the stage, grinning from ear to ear, Liam spoke up. "We did it. We really did it."

"It wasn't just about winning," Amara added, holding the trophy carefully. "It was about coming together, even when things got tough."

Sofia nodded in agreement. "We learned how to rely on each other and push through the challenges."

"And now we know what we're capable of," Ethan said with a smile.

***

Over the next few weeks, the group's friendship continued to grow. They started hanging out more often, not just to work on projects, but to enjoy each other's company. Whether it was studying together in the library, playing basketball after school, or just grabbing a bite to eat at the café, they found that they genuinely liked being around each other.

But their journey wasn't over. The success of their project had attracted attention, and soon, other students and teachers began approaching them for help with various tasks and challenges.

One day, Mr. Delgado approached them with a new opportunity. "I was impressed with your project," he said. "The school board has been discussing ways to make our school more environmentally friendly. They want a group of students to come up with ideas for sustainable practices that we can implement. Are you interested?"

Amara, Sofia, Liam, and Ethan exchanged excited looks. This was a chance to take what they had learned and apply it to something even bigger—a project that could have a lasting impact on their entire school.

"We're in," Amara said confidently.

Over the next few weeks, they dove into the project with the same passion and dedication that had driven their previous success. They researched sustainable practices, interviewed teachers and students, and brainstormed ideas for how to make the school more eco-friendly. Each member of the group brought their own unique perspective to the table:

-Amara used her scientific knowledge to propose energy-efficient systems and recycling programs.
-Sofia designed posters and campaigns to raise awareness and get students involved.
-Liam coordinated meetings and organized events, using his leadership skills to keep everyone on track.
-Ethan developed a digital platform where students could track their contributions to sustainability and learn more about the environment.

As they worked together, they realized just how much they had grown since their first project. They were no longer just individuals trying to prove themselves; they were a team with a shared goal. They had learned to trust each other's strengths and support each other through challenges. And most importantly, they had learned that they could achieve more together than they ever could alone.

One afternoon, as they were putting the finishing touches on their proposal, Liam looked around at his friends and said, "You know, I didn't think we'd come this far when we first started. But now... I can't imagine doing this without you guys."

Sofia smiled, brushing a strand of hair out of her face. "Me neither. We've really become something special."

Amara nodded, feeling a warmth in her chest that she hadn't felt before. "We're not just friends anymore. We're a team. And we can take on anything."

Ethan grinned, his usual shyness replaced with confidence. "So, what's next after this? I'm starting to think we could change the world."

***

As they continued to work on their sustainability project, the group began to realize that the skills they were developing went far beyond just schoolwork. They were learning about leadership, communication, and problem-solving in ways that would serve them throughout their lives. And more importantly, they were learning about the power of friendship and the strength that comes from unity.

Their proposal was eventually presented to the school board, and the response was overwhelmingly positive. The board approved several of their ideas, and the school began implementing new sustainability practices. The group's hard work had paid off, and they knew that they had made a real difference.

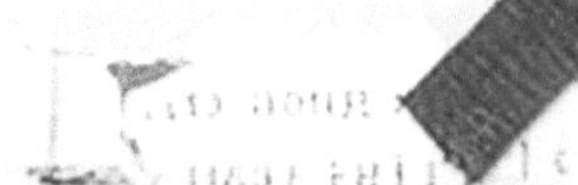

But beyond the accolades and recognition, what mattered most to them was the bond they had formed. They had started as four individuals, each with their own strengths and weaknesses, but they had become a team—a group of friends who had learned to trust and rely on each other.

As they stood in front of the school, watching as their ideas were put into action, they knew that this was just the beginning. They had faced challenges together, overcome obstacles, and achieved something they could all be proud of. And they knew that whatever came next, they would face it together.

Chapter 7: Growing Together

As summer approached, the school buzzed with end-of-year activities, from exams to graduation rehearsals. The halls were filled with excitement and a sense of anticipation for what the future held. But for Amara, Sofia, Liam, and Ethan, this time was also bittersweet. Their incredible journey together had reached a natural conclusion, yet they knew it was just the beginning of something much greater.

The impact of their work was evident throughout the school. Solar panels now dotted the rooftops, rainwater collection systems were in place, and recycling stations had become a common sight. But more than the physical changes, there was a shift in the school culture—students were more aware of their environmental footprint, more engaged in making positive changes, and more willing to work together. The team had set off a ripple effect, and they couldn't help but feel proud.

Despite their success, the group couldn't shake the feeling that something was ending. They had grown so much together, but with summer looming, they all knew that the next school year might bring changes that would separate them—different classes, new interests, and, eventually, graduation.

One evening, they decided to gather at their favorite spot, a quiet overlook just outside the town. From there, they could see the entire city spread out before them, the lights twinkling in the twilight. It was a place they had come to often, a place where they could talk freely about their dreams, fears, and everything in between.

As they sat on the grassy hill, the sun dipping below the horizon, the conversation turned reflective.

"Do you ever think about what's next?" Amara asked, her voice soft but filled with curiosity. "I mean, we've done so much this year, but what happens when we're no longer in the same classes, or when we graduate?"

The question hung in the air for a moment, heavy with the uncertainty of the future.

Sofia was the first to respond. "I think about it all the time," she admitted, twirling a blade of grass between her fingers. "It scares me, honestly. We've become such a strong team, and I don't want to lose that."

"We won't," Liam said firmly, his voice filled with conviction. "Sure, things might change. We might not see each other as much, but that doesn't mean what we've built will go away. We've created something real, something that's a part of us now."

Ethan nodded, looking up at the sky as the first stars began to appear. "Yeah, and even if we're not always together, what we've learned from each other will stay with us. The teamwork, the resilience... it's made us who we are."

Amara smiled, feeling a sense of comfort in their words. "You're right. We've been through so much together, and that's not something you just forget. It's a part of us now, like you said, Ethan."

Liam leaned back on his hands, gazing out at the city below. "This isn't the end—it's just the start of something new. We've grown together, but now it's time for us to take what we've learned and apply it to whatever comes next. And no matter where we go or what we do, we'll always have each other."

Sofia looked at her friends, feeling a deep sense of gratitude. "I'm so glad we've done this together. I can't imagine going through all of this with anyone else."

"Me neither," Amara said, her voice filled with emotion. "We've learned so much about ourselves and each other. We've faced challenges, but we've also created something beautiful."

Ethan smiled, a quiet strength in his eyes. "And that's what it's all about, right? Growing, learning, and making a difference. We're ready for whatever comes next because we've got each other's backs."

The group fell into a comfortable silence, each of them lost in their thoughts. The city lights below twinkled like a thousand possibilities, each one waiting to be explored. They knew that life would take them in different directions, but they also knew that the bond they had forged was unbreakable.

As the night deepened, Amara stood up, brushing the grass off her clothes. "You know, we should make a pact," she said, a spark of determination in her voice.

"A pact?" Liam asked, raising an eyebrow.

"Yeah," Amara continued. "No matter where we go or what we do, let's promise to keep in touch and support each other. Let's make sure that this—what we've built—never fades away."

Sofia and Ethan exchanged looks of agreement, and Liam nodded. "I'm in. No matter what happens, we stick together."

They all stood up, forming a circle, hands extended toward each other.

"To friendship, to growth, and to whatever the future holds," Amara said, her voice filled with emotion.

"To us," Sofia added, her eyes shining with unshed tears.

"Always," Ethan said, his voice steady.

"Always," Liam echoed, sealing the pact with a firm nod.

They linked hands, feeling the connection that had brought them together and would continue to unite them, no matter where life took them. The future was uncertain, but they were ready to face it, knowing that the strength they had found in each other would guide them through whatever lay ahead.

***

As the summer days passed, each of them began to pursue their individual interests, but their bond remained. They texted, called, and met up whenever they could, sharing their new experiences and challenges. Amara continued to explore her love of science, driven by a desire to make a difference in the world. Sofia's artistic talents flourished, and she began to gain recognition for her work. Liam took on new leadership roles, finding ways to bring people together, while Ethan dove deeper into technology, dreaming up innovations that could change the world.

Years later, as they prepared to graduate and move on to the next chapter of their lives, they returned to their favorite spot, just as they had done so many times before. The city lights still twinkled below, and the stars still shone above, but they were different now—stronger, wiser, and ready for whatever the world had to offer.

They sat together, reminiscing about their journey and the impact they had made. Their bond had not only endured but had grown even stronger, a testament to the power of friendship, resilience, and unity.

And as they looked out at the vast expanse of the future, they knew one thing for certain: no matter where life took them, they would always be a team. They had grown together, and that growth would continue, guiding them through the challenges and triumphs of life.

In the end, it wasn't just about the projects they had completed or the accolades they had received. It was about the journey they had shared, the lessons they had learned, and the unbreakable bond that had formed between them. It was about the strength they had found in each other, a strength that would carry them forward, no matter what the future held.

Together, they stood on the edge of tomorrow, ready to take on the world—friends, teammates, and, most importantly, a family bound not by blood, but by the love, respect, and shared experiences that had shaped them into the remarkable individuals they had become.

Epilogue:

Years later, as they went on to pursue their dreams, they continued to stay in touch, each of them finding their own path but never losing sight of the bond they had formed. And every so often, they would return to their favorite spot, standing together, just as they had done on that first night when they made their pact.

And as they looked out over the city, they knew that no matter how much time passed or how far they traveled, they would always be connected by the memories, the lessons, and the friendship that had shaped their lives.

Together, they had faced the challenges of growing up, and together, they would continue to face whatever the future held. Because in the end, they knew that the strength they had found in unity was the greatest gift they could ever give each other.

And that, above all, would be their legacy.

www.ingramcontent.com/pod-product-compliance
Lightning Source LLC
LaVergne TN
LVHW070046160826
845671LV00013B/320

* 9 7 9 8 8 9 5 6 9 4 5 9 6 *